WAYNE GRETZKY:

Portrait of a Hockey Player

7th grade reading level has been determined by using the Fry Readability Scale.

WAYNE GRETZKY: PORTRAIT OF A HOCKEY PLAYER is an original publication of Avon Books. This work has never before appeared in book form.

AVON BOOKS
A division of
The Hearst Corporation
959 Eighth Avenue
New York, New York 10019

Copyright © 1983 by Craig Thomas Wolff
Photographs Copyright © 1983 by Bruce Curtis
Photographs of Wayne Gretzky by Bruce Bennett
Published by arrangement with the author
Book design by Sheldon Winicour
Library of Congress Catalog Card Number: 82-20570
ISBN: 0-380-82420-5

Library of Congress Cataloging in Publication Data
Wolff, Craig Thomas.
    Wayne Gretzky: portrait of a hockey player.

    (An Avon/Camelot book)
    Summary: A biography of the "Great Wayne Gretzky"
of the Edmonton Oilers, who at the age of twenty-one
is already hailed as the greatest hockey player ever.
    1. Gretzky, Wayne, 1961–   . —Juvenile literature.
2. Hockey players—Canada—Biography—Juvenile litera-
ture. [1. Gretzky, Wayne, 1961–   . 2. Hockey
players]   I. Title.
GV848.5.G73W64   1983   796.96'2'0924[B]   [92]   82-20570
ISBN 0-380-82420-5

First Camelot Printing, February, 1983

Printed in the U. S. A.

DON   10   9   8   7   6   5   4   3   2   1

WAYNE GRETZKY:
Portrait of a Hockey Player

Craig Thomas Wolff

Photographed by Bruce Curtis

with photographs of Wayne Gretzky by Bruce Bennett

AN AVON CAMELOT BOOK

It was the kind of night of which dreams are made. With just a little more than six minutes left in the hockey game, Wayne Gretzky of the Edmonton Oilers got that special feeling. It is the feeling he always gets right before he scores a goal.

Gretzky was seeking his 77th goal of the season. It would be the record for most goals in a single season in the history of hockey.

Aiming for the record

Holding the puck with his hockey stick, Gretzky first skated past one defender, and then another. All that stood between Gretzky and the record was the goaltender for the Buffalo Sabres. Gretzky wasted no time. When he reached a point about 10 feet away from the goal, he shot the puck. The puck moved so fast, the goaltender didn't even see it. It went right through his legs.

Gretzky was seeking his 77th goal of the season.

The scoring record belonged to Gretzky. The fans cheered. They stood and clapped for several minutes to show their appreciation. Gretzky—or the Great Gretzky as his fans call him—waved to the crowd. He knew he had made hockey history. Before the night was over, Gretzky scored two more goals. His team, the Oilers, won 6–3.

That was February 24, 1982. The city was Buffalo. It was a great night for the Great Gretzky. He is used to great nights. In each of the last three years, Gretzky has been named hockey's MVP. MVP stands for Most Valuable Player.

Most players don't become stars until they are about 28 years old. Gretzky is only 21. He is the greatest player in the game today. He is probably the greatest hockey player—ever. For the Great Gretzky, it is a dream come true.

Dreams are not made in one day or one night. It takes years of hard work. For Wayne Gretzky, the dream began when he was two years old. His family lived in a small city named Brantford. Brantford is in the province of Ontario, which is in Canada. Most hockey players come from Canada. Wayne's father, Walter, built a tiny ice rink in the backyard. Wayne learned how to skate there. He skated back and forth day after day. He also practiced passing the puck. He practiced shooting the puck into the goal. When Wayne got a little older, he would practice with friends from the neighborhood. He also practiced with his three younger brothers.

On ice Gretzky moved like a cat.

Some say Gretzky is a great player because he learned so young. Others say he was born with natural talent. Walter Gretzky, Wayne's dad, once explained his son's ability this way:

"The minute he put on skates, I could tell he had talent. Wayne moved on the ice with confidence. But success has not come easily. He has had to work, work, work."

As a young boy, Wayne practiced early in the morning before school. When he was six years old, he played on his first team. Everyone else on the team was 10 or 11 years old.

On ice, Gretzky moved like a cat. He was very, very quick. People began to notice this skinny little kid. When Wayne was seven, he was interviewed on television. By the time he was nine years old, all of Canada had heard of Gretzky. When he was 11, he scored 378 goals in 68 games. That's more than five goals a game. Hockey games are 60 minutes long. Once in a game, Gretzky scored 3 goals in 45 seconds.

When Wayne was 14, he played on a team away from home. He lived and went to school with other young hockey players. He was homesick, but he played on. At 16, he moved to the Junior A level. In Canada, there are many levels of hockey before a player becomes a professional. The name of Gretzky's Junior A team was the Sault Ste. Marie Greyhounds. Most of the players on the team were at least three years older than Wayne. He became the team's leading scorer. He scored 54 goals and had 87 assists in his first 48 games. A player gets an assist when he helps a teammate score a goal. Gretzky gets a lot of assists also. That's what makes him so great. Even when he is not scoring, he can help his team with assists.

Gretzky has always played the center position. The center is usually the most important man on the team. The two forwards try to score most of the time. The two defensemen try to stop the other team from scoring. The goaltender tries to stop the other team from scoring. But the center has to do everything. He has to score. He has to stop the opponent from scoring. And he has to pass the puck.

Gretzky does all these things well. He always seems to know what to do with the puck. He can skate and pass the puck and never have to look down or sideways. He always knows where his teammates are in case he has to pass to them. No one else in hockey can do all these things.

How did Gretzky become so great. How did he learn? How can you learn? There are ways—special ways to practice.

The most important skill in hockey is skating. Always make sure your skates fit well. Make sure the blades are always clean. This will help you move easily on the ice. Use long, smooth strides when you skate. And keep your knees apart and your legs apart.

Most important, don't be scared of the ice. Beginners should practice leg lifts and jumps. These exercises are good for stretching your muscles. They are also good for making you unafraid of the ice.

The center is the most important man on the team.

Leg-lifts

Leg-lifts

Leg-lifts

Jumps

A hockey player should always skate with his head up. He should stay alert. The Great Gretzky has always skated this way. Brad Park of the Boston Bruins once said about Gretzky: "He always sees what is happening all over the ice. Sometimes I think he has eyes in the back of his head." Gretzky doesn't have eyes in the back of his head, but his eyes are always moving. That helps him see more, and that's important in hockey. It is such a fast game. The action can become like a blur. So remember: head up and eyes moving.

Since a good hockey player has to skate very fast, he often has to stop very fast. The best way to stop is to turn sideways and then dig your front skate sideways into the ice. This has to be done very quickly.

Stopping

Practicing can be hard and tiring. It helps to have people to learn with. If you have brothers as Gretzky has, skate with them. Or learn with your friends.

Stickhandling is another important part of hockey. Stickhandling is really keeping and moving the puck on the end of the stick. The end of the stick is also called the blade of the stick. If you are good at skating and good at stickhandling, it will help your team score goals. And just like Gretzky, it would be even better if you could pass well too.

Hockey players often call a player who knows how to pass a player with good sense. An excellent passer seems to have a sense of when to pass the puck and when to hold on to the puck. The idea is to always keep the puck moving. If the puck stays still, the other team will take it away. If the puck is constantly moving and going from one teammate to the other, your opponent will not be able to keep up with you.

If you pass the puck to your teammate and he scores, you get an assist. Add your goals scored and your assists and you get your total points. We now know that Gretzky scored more goals last year than anyone ever had before. He also set the record for assists and the record for total points. Gretzky is a great shooter. He knows how to put the puck past the other team's goaltender and into the net. His passing deserves just as much attention. So does your passing. Remember that the best teams know how to pass.

There are two kinds of passing. There are forehand passes and backhand passes. If you pass the puck ahead of yourself, that is a forehand pass. If you pass it behind yourself, it is a backhand pass. Don't slap at the puck. If you push the puck to your teammate, you will have more control. A good passer doesn't use his arms. He uses his wrists by twisting and turning suddenly. Everything in hockey depends on quickness. That goes for your legs, your eyes, and even your wrists.

If you pass the puck, someone has to receive it. Hopefully, it will be someone on *your* team. When receiving a pass, make sure the blade of your stick is against the ice. When the pass comes, move the stick back just a bit. This way, the puck won't bounce off the stick. The pros like to say that a good pass receiver knows how to cradle the puck like it's a baby.

Passing the puck

What makes Gretzky such a complete player is that he keeps moving when receiving the puck. He doesn't give the other team time to think. There are ways to practice this. With a teammate or more than one teammate, practice passing. Skate up and down the rink, pushing the puck to one another. Try passing between large cones. Soon, you will not have to look at the puck. What once was hard work will come naturally.

Passing drills

The goaltender

If you keep moving and passing, it will soon be time to try to score. To do this you have to get the puck past the opponent's goaltender. This is not easy. The goaltender stands in front of the net. He doesn't skate up and down the ice. And he is allowed to catch the puck with his hands. The goaltender wears special equipment to protect himself from flying

A shot on goal

pucks. He wears large gloves for his hands. He also wears extra padding for his body. Like all players, he wears a helmet. And he wears a mask over his face. He can see out of the mask, but the pucks can't get in. With all this equipment, the goaltender looks like a creature from outer space.

Another shot

Goal!

Save!

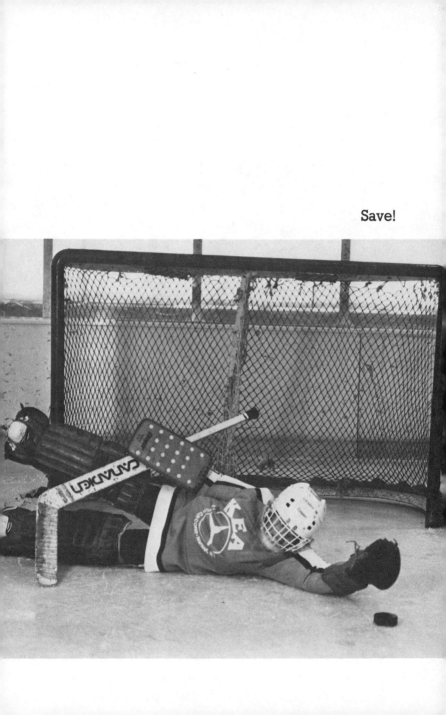

The idea in scoring is to fool the goaltender. Make him think you will shoot the puck to his left and then shoot it to the right. As you might have guessed, Gretzky does this very well. Glenn Resch, a goaltender for the New Jersey Devils, once said: "Gretzky knows how to trick the goaltender. One second the puck is on his stick, the next second it is gone. The puck is in the net, and the goaltender is lying on the ice. Gretzky can shoot that puck."

Another goal

Shooting the puck is an art. The lower hand on the stick gives power to your shot. The upper hand helps you to aim the shot. Basically, there are two kinds of shots. The wrist shot is the most tricky. It is done without lifting the blade of your stick up from the ice. With a quick turn of the wrists, you can score. And remember that most important lesson. Don't keep your eyes on the puck. Look at that net, or goal, and aim.

"I know what makes Gretzky so great," says Glen Sather, Wayne's coach on the Oilers. "He imagines what he wants to do with the puck. He actually pictures the puck going in the net. He pictures it in his mind. Then his body does what his mind wants it to."

Holding the stick properly

The second kind of shot, the slap shot, is probably at the heart of Wayne's game. Most players can't always make the slap shot go where they want it to. It is a wilder shot than the wrist shot. How do you do the slap shot? First, make sure both feet are firmly set on the ice. Bring your stick slightly in back of you, up off the ice. Then swing the stick down toward the puck. Keep the stick moving forward—even after hitting the puck. On the slap shot, break the rule of not looking at the puck. Look at the puck, or else your stick will hit nothing but air.

Slap shot

Strong wrists make a strong hockey player. That's the old saying in hockey. Strong wrists can help your passing and shooting become stronger. Believe it or not, there are exercises for the wrists. Squeezing rubber balls or tennis balls can help. Lifting weights can also do the job.

Of course, most coaches advise you to keep the rest of your body in shape. Such exercises as the twist stick are good for you. Hold the stick behind your back and simply twist back and forth. Off the ice, push-ups, sit-ups, and running will firm up your muscles.

Twist stick

Now that you know how to play hockey, how do you begin the game? Which team gets the puck first? That's what a face-off is for. The centers of both teams stand facing each other in the center of the rink. The referee drops the puck between them and the centers battle for the puck. They battle by banging their sticks together.

Face-off

Action during face-off

A problem in hockey today is that players often battle with their fists. This should not be copied. Even the players who fight on the ice don't like it. Hockey is such a fast game they say that they get caught up in the heat of the moment.

Player in penalty box

Fighting also hurts your own team. If you start a fight, or trip another player with your stick, or actually hit him with your stick, you will be put in the penalty box. The penalty box is alongside the rink. You will have to stay there for two minutes or five minutes. Your team will have to play with one fewer man. If you make a very bad penalty, the referee may force you to leave the game.

End of the game

Gretzky is known for playing a "clean game." That is, he doesn't get many penalties. "I don't like penalties," he has said. "The penalty box is not a happy place to be. And besides, how can I score goals when I'm sitting in the box?"

That last statement says it all for Gretzky. He is the team man. He is happy to have set records, but unhappy that his team, the Oilers, has not won the Stanley Cup. The Stanley Cup is actually a large gold cup. It is given as a reward for winning the championship of the National Hockey League.

Hockey's Man of the Year, Wayne, once said, "I have dreamed of winning the Stanley Cup ever since I became a professional."

Incredibly, Gretzky became a professional when he was only 17 years old. He signed a contract with the Indianapolis Racers of the World Hockey Association. This league no longer exists. The contract paid him almost a million dollars. Some of the players on the team were twice as old as Gretzky.

It turned out that the Racers didn't have enough money to pay Gretzky. They sold his contract to the Edmonton Oilers, who were also in the World Hockey Association. Immediately, Gretzky did well. In one of his first games, he scored a "hat trick." A hat trick is when a player scores three goals in one game. Gretzky was a hit. He signed a contract with the Oilers that will last him his entire career.

Some people argued that Gretzky was really not that good. They wanted to see if he could play in the better league, the National Hockey League.

In the 1979–1980 season, these non-believers got their wish. Four teams from the WHA joined the NHL. The Oilers were one of these teams. For his first season, in the NHL, Gretzky promised himself that he would score as many goals in his first season in the NHL as he had in the WHA. He knew that if he didn't, people would say, "Gretzky's good, but he's not *that* good."

Wayne ended up doing better than even he expected. He tied for most points in the league—137. He won the Lady Byng Trophy. The Lady Byng trophy is given to the player who gets the fewest penalties. And last but not least, he won the Most Valuable Player award.

The next season, Gretzky scored 164 points. No one had ever gotten that many. In the playoffs that year, Gretzky dazzled. In the first game, against the Montreal Canadiens, Gretzky scored five goals. Even the Montreal players said that they could not believe their eyes. In the second game, Gretzky had a goal and two assists. The Oilers won the second game, 3–1. And they won the next game, 6–2. When Gretzky was on the ice in the playoff games, the Oilers scored 11 goals. The Canadiens didn't score any.

In the next round of the playoffs, the Oilers lost to the New York Islanders. There was no shame in that. The Islanders are the champions of hockey. Still, Gretzky was upset. "I don't like losing," he said.

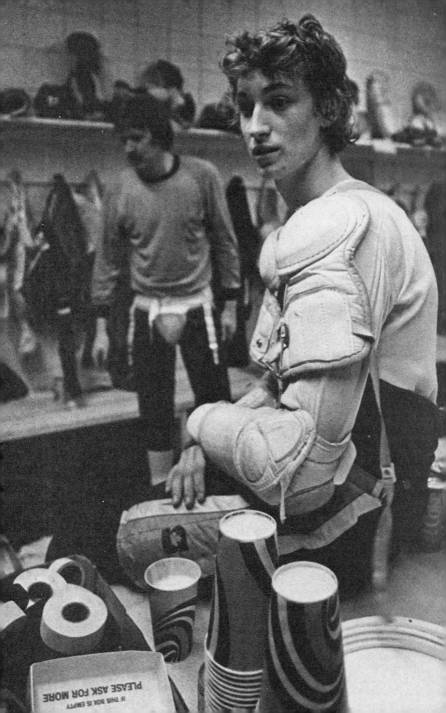

In the 1981–1982 season, Gretzky broke all the records. Most goals—92. Most assists—120. Most points—212. No one had ever thought it was possible for a player to get more than 200 points. The question is: how will Gretzky top this? "By winning the Stanley cup," he says.

Gretzky is paid a lot of money, close to a million dollars each year. He makes even more money by doing TV commercials. He also gets paid for putting his name on different products. His name appears on hockey sticks, hockey gloves, pens, and hockey helmets. He gets paid by the companies that make these products.

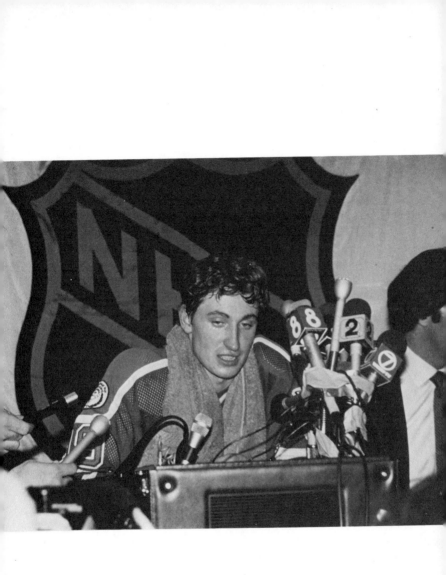

There is even a pants company which named its jeans after Wayne. It is called GWG. GWG stands for Great Wayne Gretzky. Wayne even gets letters from girls who ask him if he would marry them. He always politely says no. At the moment he is not married. He does have a steady girlfriend.

His coach, Glen Sather, worries that all these activities will distract Wayne from the most important thing—hockey. So far that hasn't happened. Some players who make a lot of money don't play so hard. But Wayne works as hard as he ever has.

Wayne has an agent who handles all the business activities. And his family reminds him that he is still only 21 years old. His mother and father make sure that Wayne doesn't get a big head. Even Wayne worries that people around him will be jealous of him. His teammate on the Oilers, Mark Messier, has said: "That will never happen. Wayne is too nice a guy."

Wayne seems to get along with all of his teammates. He is much younger than most of them. He is used to that. When he first became a professional, his teammates would go have a few beers after games. Wayne could not join them. He was too young to drink alcohol.

He is also smaller than most. When he joined the Oilers, he weighed only 160 pounds. When people met him and another teammate at the same time they would think that Wayne was the other player's younger brother. Wayne looked that young.

Gretzky laughs about looking so young. He has said: "The only thing that matters to me is playing good hockey. Not how I look."

It has always been all business on the ice. His father told him when he was very young that he should always work hard.

"Don't worry about girls and cars and money," his father told Wayne. "You will get all that if you work hard. Hard work is everything."

That has been the Great Gretzky's motto. Hard work makes for the best hockey player. Meanwhile, people are wondering, what next? Gretzky has many years left to play. If he is so great at the age of 21, how much greater will he become? No one knows the answer. Not even Gretzky. The best may be yet to come.

Hockey Words to Know

ASSIST: Credit for making a pass to a teammate who then scores a goal.

BLADE: Either the bottom of your skate or the tip of your stick.

CHECKING: Guarding an opposing player very closely.

DIGGING FOR THE PUCK: Battling for a puck among a crowd of players.

FACE-OFF: The method used to start play at the beginning of each period, after a goal has been scored, or after any other stoppage of play. The referee drops the puck between the two centers, who then battle for it.

GOAL: A point scored when you send the puck into the opposition's goal (or net).

HAT TRICK: When one player scores three goals in one game.

NHL: The National Hockey League

PENALTY BOX: A small area alongside the rink where players sit for having made a penalty.

REBOUND: A puck that bounces off a goaltender back into scoring position.

SAVE: When the goaltender stops a shot and prevents the score.

SHOT ON GOAL: A shot that heads toward the goaltender.

SLAP SHOT: A very strong shot, made by lifting the stick first up and back, and then down toward the puck.

STICKHANDLING: The art of moving the puck with the blade of your stick.

WRIST SHOT: A shot made with a sudden turn of the wrists and without lifting the stick off the ice.